ACID RAIN

© Aladdin Books Ltd

Designed and produced by
Aladdin Books Ltd
70 Old Compton Street
London W1

*First published in
the United States in 1986 by*
Gloucester Press
387 Park Avenue South
New York NY 10016

ISBN 0 531 17016 0

Library of Congress Catalog
Card Number: 85-81981

Printed in Belgium

The front cover photograph shows trees blighted by acid rain in West Germany. The back cover photograph shows smog in Mexico City.

Contents

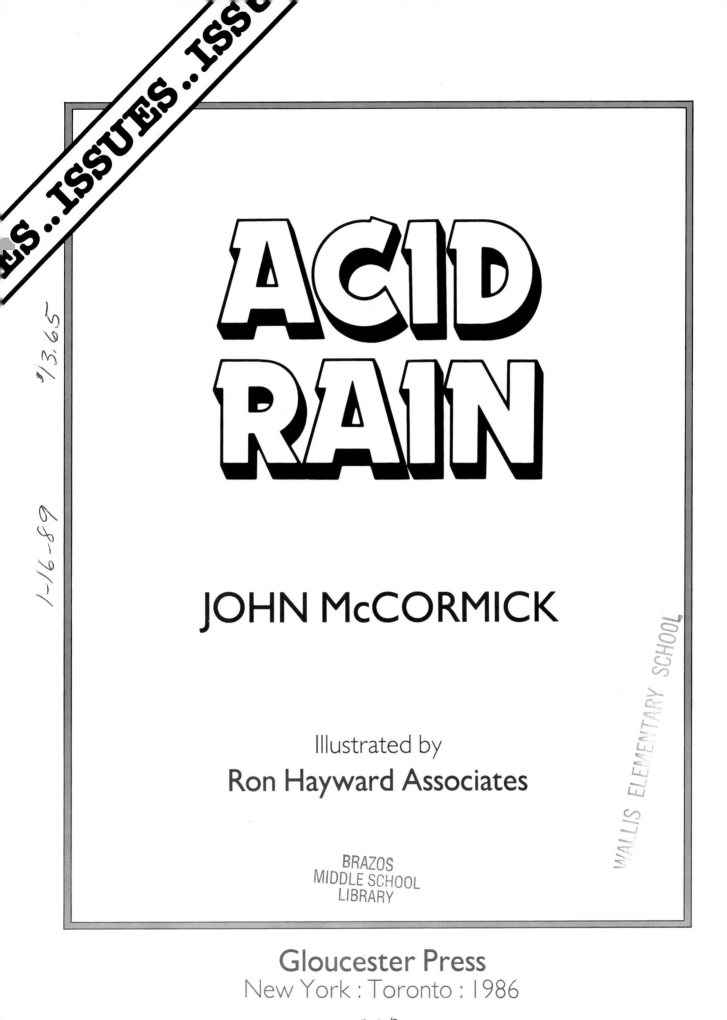

ACID RAIN

JOHN McCORMICK

Illustrated by

Ron Hayward Associates

Gloucester Press
New York : Toronto : 1986

Introduction

An acid blight is spreading across the Earth. Rain, snow, fog and mist, polluted by the smoke and fumes given off by factories and cars, are being turned acid. This "acid rain" is gradually wearing down our environment, affecting countries in almost every continent. It attacks and damages our buildings and monuments. Forests are dead or dying. Soils are turning acid, wildlife dying, crops are being lost. Lakes are emptying as their populations perish in rising acid levels.

In cities throughout the world, people are choking – even dying – from the effects of acid smoke and pollution.

Acid rain is not a new problem, but it is now severe and obvious enough to cause concern. In fact, it has become one of the most serious of all environmental problems. Yet although we know how it is caused, scientists are still not sure exactly how it damages the environment. In this book we will look at what acid rain is, why acid pollution is a problem, and what can be done to control it.

People who live in the sprawling city of Los Angeles, California, depend heavily on their cars. But fumes given off by these cars are part of the reason why the city has so many choking smogs.

Polluted skies

Acid pollution is caused by the smoke and gases given off by things like factories, cars and trucks, that run on fossil fuels like coal and oil.

When the fuels are burned to produce energy, two side effects occur. The sulfur naturally present in the fuel combines with oxygen and becomes sulfur dioxide, and some of the nitrogen in the air, and in the fuel itself, turns into nitrogen oxides. These pollutants pour into the atmosphere along with smoke.

In the atmosphere, these oxides undergo further changes and become acid. They return to earth, either as "dry deposition" (gases and particles, most of which fall locally,) or they combine with the water in the atmosphere to form dilute sulfuric acid and nitric acid, which fall to the ground as "wet deposition" (acid rain, snow, mist and fog.)

Nowadays, only about half the sulfur dioxide occurring in the atmosphere is natural; it comes from volcanoes, swamps and other rotting organic material. The rest is manmade. And in industrial regions, the proportion of manmade sulfur dioxide in the air can be as high as 90 percent.

unnatural 90%   natural 10%

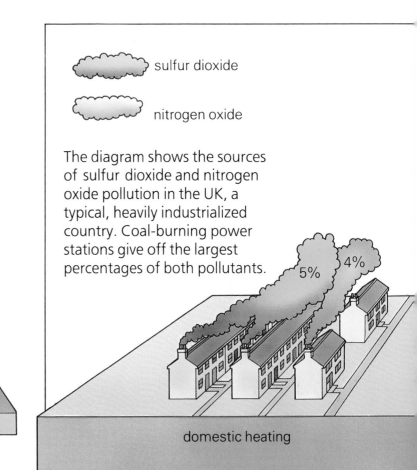

sulfur dioxide

nitrogen oxide

The diagram shows the sources of sulfur dioxide and nitrogen oxide pollution in the UK, a typical, heavily industrialized country. Coal-burning power stations give off the largest percentages of both pollutants.

5%   4%

domestic heating

As pollutants enter the atmosphere, we see acid rain in the making

66%

28%

21%

29%

46%

1%

commerce and industry

vehicles

power stations

Acid dust

Many of the fumes given off by power stations, smelters, houses and cars do not rise very far into the air and return to earth almost immediately as dry deposition.

Settling back on the ground, this proceeds to attack and corrode buildings and stonework, and shorten the working life of metals and paintwork. It can even damage leather, paper and cloth indoors. Fumes can be blown by winds onto nearby forests and farmlands, damaging trees, stunting plant growth and reducing crop yields — and can cause millions of dollars worth of damage. And they can help form another kind of pollutant, called "ozone," which is particularly harmful in combination with other pollutants.

▽ Industry is a vital source of jobs, income and goods. But factories can offset these benefits by pumping noxious fumes into the air, polluting the environment and threatening human health.

These pollutants also mix with fog and dust to create smog that may harm the very young and the very old and people suffering from breathing problems or weak hearts. Big cities like Los Angeles, Athens and Mexico City are infamous for their smogs.

London used to have serious smogs: in 1952 a winter smog hastened the deaths of around 4,000 people, causing the government to take steps to control air pollution. London now has cleaner air than many other cities.

▽ Ozone, a form of oxygen, occurs naturally in the atmosphere, and shields us from ultraviolet radiation. But, on warm days chemicals called hydrocarbons (from vehicle exhausts) react with nitrogen oxide from various sources, to form an unnatural ozone at ground level. This ozone is a pollutant in its own right, but can combine with others.

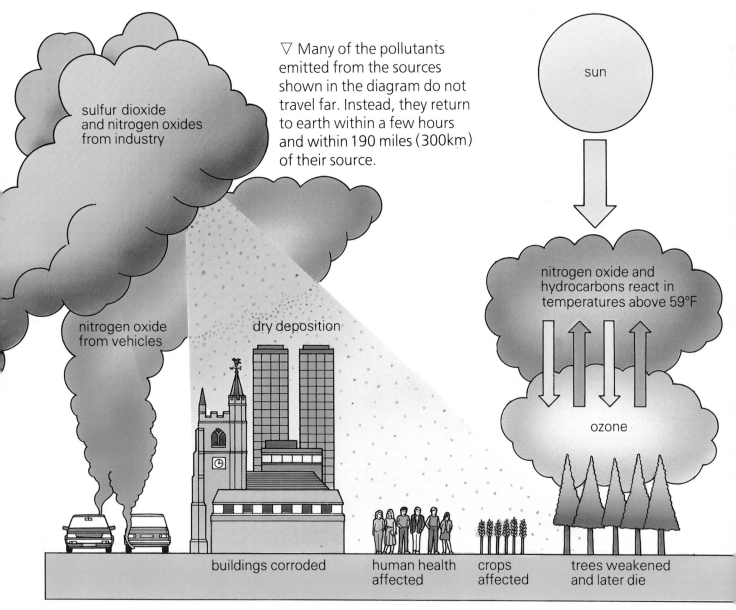

▽ Many of the pollutants emitted from the sources shown in the diagram do not travel far. Instead, they return to earth within a few hours and within 190 miles (300km) of their source.

sulfur dioxide and nitrogen oxides from industry

nitrogen oxide from vehicles

dry deposition

sun

nitrogen oxide and hydrocarbons react in temperatures above 59°F

ozone

buildings corroded

human health affected

crops affected

trees weakened and later die

Acid rain

The longer pollutants stay in the atmosphere, the greater the chances of their reacting with moisture to form acid precipitations, or wet deposition. With a strong wind, the oxides and acids can stay in the atmosphere for several days and be carried many hundreds of miles, often across national frontiers.

Wet deposition – like dry deposition – can damage the environment in several ways. It can directly attack the leaves and needles on trees. It can soak into soil, affecting its chemical balance and so damaging plants and crops. It can run off into rivers and lakes, polluting drinking water and killing aquatic animal and plant life. And it can also attack stonework.

▽ Pollutants in the air sometimes combine with water in the clouds to form dilute sulfuric and nitric acids. This is the true acid rain – or fog, or snow. Its effects can be disastrous.

sulfur and nitrogen oxides

chemical reactions with moisture in the atmosphere

sulfuric and nitric acids formed

acid rain

▷ Some acid pollutants can be carried more than 620 miles (1000 km) by the wind, so the damage caused can actually occur far away from the source of the pollution. It may even occur in a different country.

vegetation affected

soil affected

lakes affected

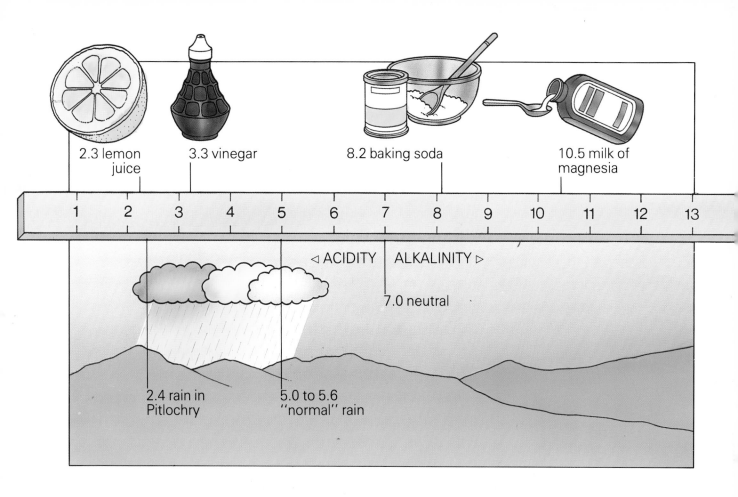

2.3 lemon juice

3.3 vinegar

8.2 baking soda

10.5 milk of magnesia

| 1 | 2 | 3 | 4 | 5 | 6 | 7 | 8 | 9 | 10 | 11 | 12 | 13 |

◁ ACIDITY | ALKALINITY ▷

7.0 neutral

2.4 rain in Pitlochry

5.0 to 5.6 "normal" rain

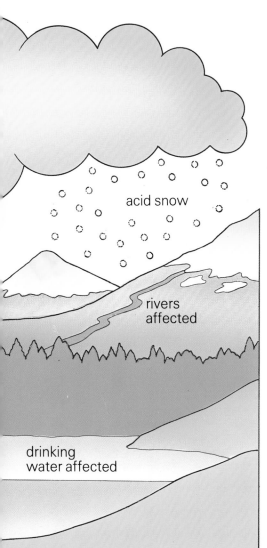

acid snow

rivers affected

drinking water affected

△ The pH scale is used for measuring levels of acidity and alkalinity. It ranges from 0-14, and the lower the pH value, the more acid the liquid. The scale is logarithmic. This means that pH5 is ten times stronger than pH6, pH4 a hundred times stronger, pH3 a thousand times, and so on. The most polluted rain — like that which fell on Pitlochry, Scotland in 1974 — can be as acid as lemon juice.

All rain is slightly acid anyway — carbon dioxide naturally present in air dissolves in rain water to form a light acid. This is actually useful, because it helps dissolve minerals in soil, so that they can be taken up more easily by plants and consequently by animals.

But higher levels of acid become destructive. The acidity of rain in parts of Europe and North America has suddenly and dramatically increased over the past few decades. Rain that is between ten and seventy times more acid than unpolluted rain is now common in many places. We know this as we can measure acidity on the "pH" scale shown here.

Naked forests

Forests are among the most valuable of the Earth's natural resources; they regulate local climate, store and distribute water, bind soil, are home to a wealth of wildlife, and not least, supply our timber.

But forests are dying all across Europe and North America. Nearly 6.7 million hectares (16.5 million acres) of forest are damaged or dying in six European countries alone: West Germany, East Germany, Austria, Poland, Czechoslovakia and Romania.

While there are many theories, it seems certain acid pollution is one of the major causes of the damage. Damaged trees lose their needles or leaves, suffer from stunted growth, and have damaged bark, making them vulnerable to attacks from harsh weather, insects and disease. The worst affected trees are conifers.

1982	1983	1984
7.4%	34%	50.2%

△ Surveys in West Germany show how rapidly forest damage is spreading. In 1982, less than 8 percent of trees (1 in 12) were affected. By 1984, more than half the country's forests showed clear signs of having been damaged by acid rain.

▷ Forests in Scandinavia are being damaged by acid rain. The map shows how sulfur pollution is imported from a large number of countries: 82 percent of Sweden's acid rain is due to foreign pollution.

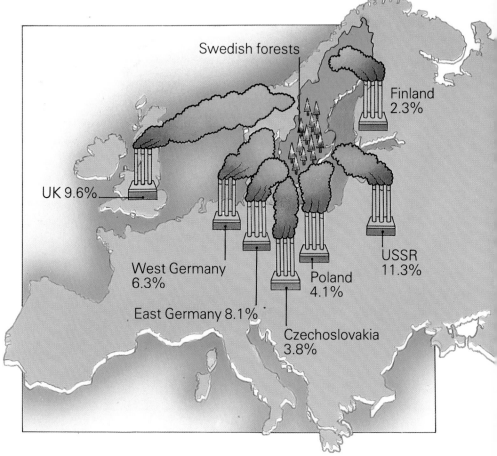

Swedish forests

Finland
2.3%

UK 9.6%

West Germany
6.3%

East Germany 8.1%

Poland
4.1%

Czechoslovakia
3.8%

USSR
11.3%

Acid damaged trees
in the Vosges, France

alkalines from the soil taken up to neutralize acidity on the leaves

When acid rain falls onto its leaves, a tree will absorb alkalines from the soil, to counter the effect of the acid. As a result, the soil becomes more acid. Rain falling directly onto the soil also increases its acidity. Acid water moves through the soil, washing out nutrients and releasing poisonous metals, some of which are absorbed by the tree roots. It can be many years before the damage begins to show, and by then a whole forest may be affected.

poisonous metals are released and absorbed by the roots

alkaline

rain increases the soil's acidity

nutrients are washed away

Poisoned soil

To understand the plight of the forest, we have to look at the soil. Soil is one of the richest and most valuable of all the Earth's natural resources, supporting crops and forests. Deep soils that are rich in certain minerals can "neutralize" the acid rain that seeps into them, canceling out the acidity by making the water alkaline. But thin, sandy soils do not absorb water, so acid rain will wash straight off them and into rivers and lakes.

Plants and soils live in a complex natural system, where nutrients (chemicals that nourish plants), are taken up from the soil and then returned to the soil. If the soil is affected by acid pollution, this cycle is upset. This in turn can kill off the vegetation. Damage to soil is the most serious effect of acid rain.

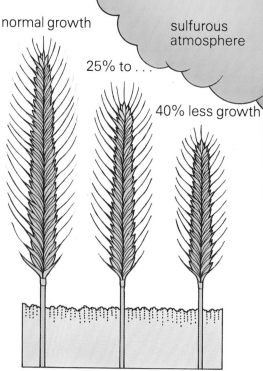

normal growth

sulfurous atmosphere

25% to . . .

40% less growth

△ Several crops are sensitive to air pollution. Research has indicated that the growth of rye grass and barley, for example, decreases by 25 to 40 percent in sulfurous atmospheres.

◁ Tobacco plants can be affected by ozone. Until the 1950s, the damage — which shows first on the leaves — was called "weather fleck." Now we know that it is ozone damage.

15

Sinister beauty

A lake damaged by acid pollution looks oddly beautiful. Because most of the life in the lake is dead, and because dust and sediment are often trapped on the lake bed by certain mosses that can survive in acid, the water becomes crystal clear.

But this beauty is deceptive – a lifeless lake is like a desert. Some species, like fish, can adapt to the acidity in the water for a time, but once the acidity reaches a certain level, all but the most resilient animals and plants disappear. These effects have been noted in lakes as far apart as Canada and Sweden. Lakes are attacked by acid deposition in several ways.

▽ A healthy lake supports a wealth of wildlife, from birds on the shore to insects and lilies on the surface, and fish, mollusks, plants and plankton below the surface.

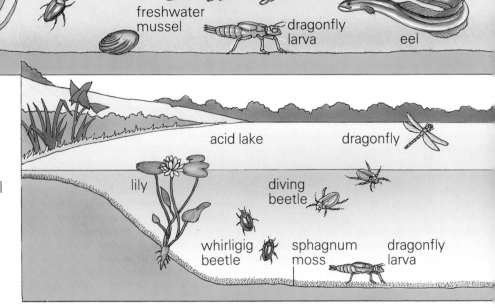

heron

lily

healthy lake

dragonfly

roach

diving beetle

pike

perch

snail

whirligig beetle

freshwater mussel

dragonfly larva

eel

acid lake

dragonfly

lily

diving beetle

whirligig beetle

sphagnum moss

dragonfly larva

▷ An acid polluted lake supports only the hardiest and most resistant species. Fish will die off, removing the main source of food for birds. Birds will die from eating insect larvae that have absorbed toxic aluminum from the acidified water.

Acid water flows in from rivers, washes off surrounding land or falls directly into the lake as acid rain, snow or dust. Moreover, toxic metals released from the soil by acid ground water, are washed into the lakes. One of the most toxic of these metals is aluminum, which kills fish by interfering with their breathing.

The most dangerous time for lakes in northern Europe and North America is during the spring, when snow begins to melt and runs off into lakes and rivers. Acid that has built up in the snow over the winter causes a sudden rise in the acidity of lakes, killing the fish. Salmon and trout are particularly at risk when this happens.

▽ There is a way of controlling acidity in lakes. By pouring in tons of lime, the acid can be neutralized. But this is short-term, difficult and expensive, and controls the symptoms rather than the causes of acid pollution.

Corrosion

▽ The Parthenon is seriously corroded. Experts say that pollution has caused more damage to the Parthenon in the past 20-25 years, than it sustained from natural forces in the previous 2,400 years. The worst pollution has been caused by exhaust fumes from vehicles and by local industry.

vehicles

factories

heating

Soft building stones have always been naturally corroded by the effects of rain and wind, but in recent years – thanks to acid pollution – the amount of damage has leaped considerably.

Famous buildings like the Parthenon in Athens, the Statue of Liberty in New York, St Paul's Cathedral in London, and the Taj Mahal in India have all been damaged by air pollution. Much of the corrosion is caused by dry deposition. When sulfur pollutants fall on the surfaces of buildings made from sandstone or limestone, for example, they react with minerals in the stone to form gypsum, a powdery substance that can be washed away by rain.

But buildings are not the only things that are affected. Acid pollution has even corroded stained glass, railroad lines, steel bridges, underground pipes – and cars themselves.

△ Damaged figures on the Erechtheum near the Parthenon

Effects of acid corrosion on a church in Surrey, UK

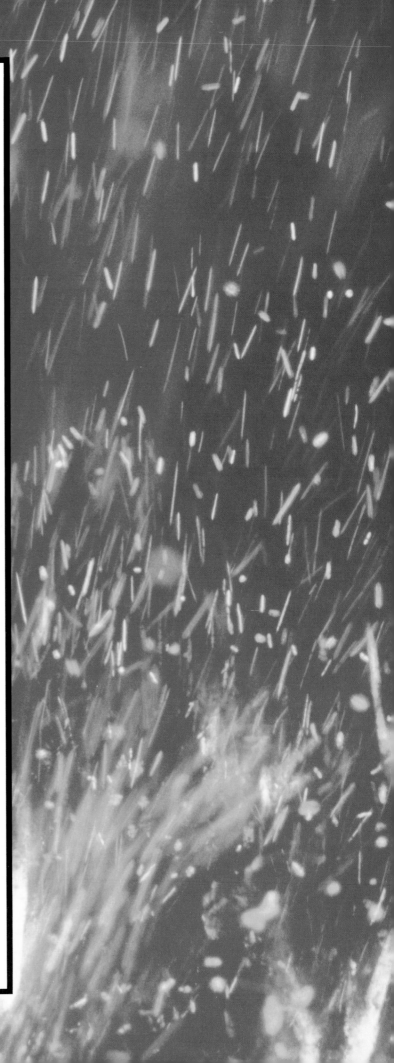

In fluidized bed combustion, coal is burned in a chamber containing limestone, and air is blown through the chamber. The coal floats in the air, and sulfur is absorbed by the limestone. This reduces the amount of harmful oxides in the gas given off, by up to 90 percent.

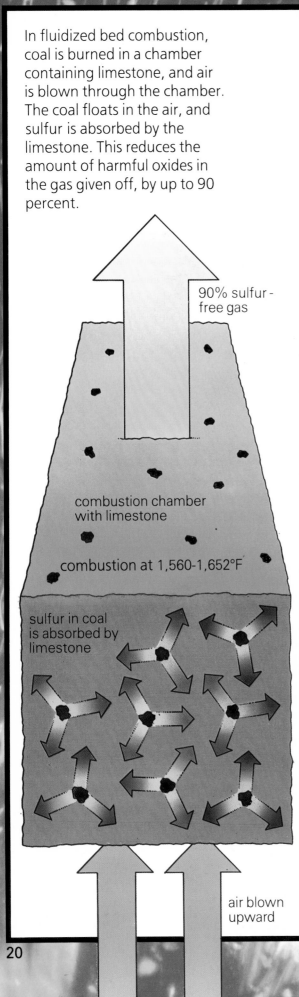

90% sulfur-free gas

combustion chamber with limestone

combustion at 1,560–1,652°F

sulfur in coal is absorbed by limestone

air blown upward

Solutions

Acid pollution is a serious problem, but there are several well-tried ways of bringing it under control and cleaning or reducing the smoke and ash that cause the damage.

One of the simplest ways is to clean coal before it is burned. It is crushed and then washed in water or passed through an electrostatic process that takes out the sulfur. Sulfur can be taken out of oil by refining or distilling it in a vacuum and then reacting it with hydrogen.

The way fuels are burned can be controlled to reduce the amount of sulfur and nitrogen oxides they release. Sulfur can be taken out with a process called "fluidized bed combustion." Because nitrogen oxides are formed by burning fuels reacting with nitrogen in the air, they can be reduced by lowering the combustion temperature and reducing the time air stays in the combustion chamber. However, replacing existing techniques with new ones costs money.

▽ In 1976, coal cleaning cut the amount of sulfur produced in the industrial northeastern states of the USA by nearly 2.5 million tons. If *all* the coal used there were treated, twice as much sulfur again (or, a fifth of all the sulfur produced by the United States), could be cleaned out.

Cleaner smoke

Even after combustion, acid pollution can still be reduced by filtering the smoke and gases given off by power stations, factories and cars.

The exhaust gases given off by factories can be cleaned by treating them with chemicals. Gases given off by cars and trucks can be cleaned by fitting filters, called "catalytic converters," to the exhaust system, or by using a special lean-burn engine, that reduces the amount of gas given off.

Another way of reducing acid pollution is by conserving energy. Every time we turn on an electric light switch, we are helping to create acid rain. We waste heat because our homes are drafty. Experts have calculated that in some countries, if energy were used more carefully, we could halve the amount of fuel we burned. This too would mean a big reduction in the amount of harmful oxides produced by burning fuel.

calcium sulfite produced

calcium sulfite sludge

calcium sulfite is oxidized to form gypsum

lime and water in

smoke in

gypsum

The most common way of reducing the emission of sulfur-based pollutants in factories, involves the use of a chemical process. Exhaust gases, or "flue gases," are brought into contact with a chemical as they pass through the factory chimney. This chemical absorbs the sulfur in the gases. This is called "flue gas desulfurization."

A case for treatment. Soon to be cured?

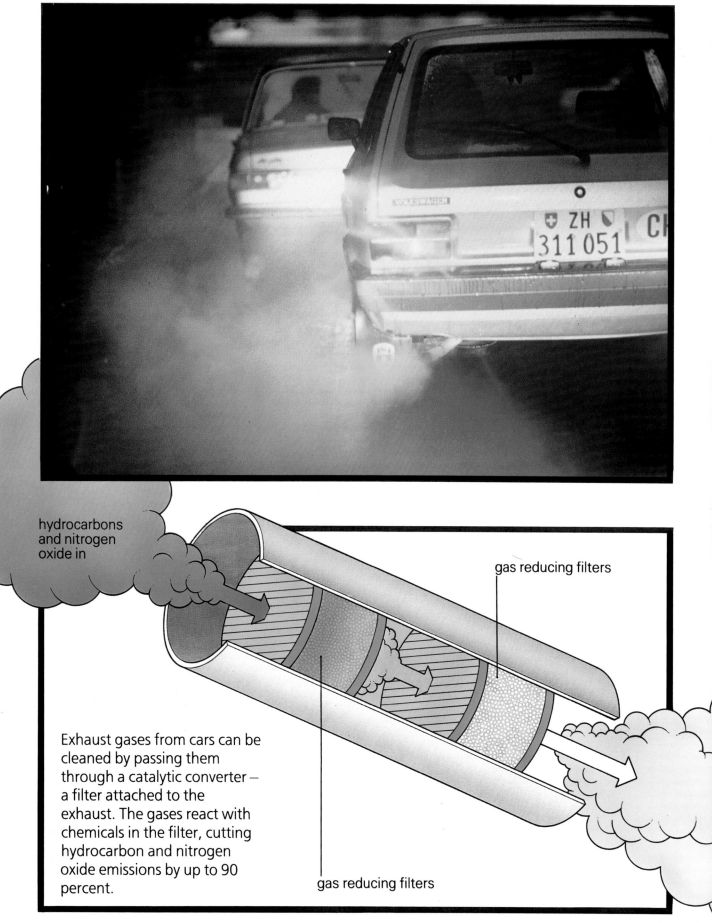

hydrocarbons and nitrogen oxide in

gas reducing filters

Exhaust gases from cars can be cleaned by passing them through a catalytic converter – a filter attached to the exhaust. The gases react with chemicals in the filter, cutting hydrocarbon and nitrogen oxide emissions by up to 90 percent.

gas reducing filters

Acid trade

One of the consequences of acid rain being carried across national frontiers is that it causes ill-feeling between countries.

One example of this is in North America, where pollution from the major industrial areas of the northeastern United States is carried into Canada. Further south, pollution from huge metal smelters in northern Mexico is carried north to the Rocky Mountains of the United States, where it is turning lakes acid.

In Europe some governments are strangely reluctant to admit the extent of the damage done to their forests — possibly because the truth might harm their timber industries. Others not only admit the damage, but name the countries they hold responsible.

▽ At least one expert claims that if the truth were known, *all* the trees in the middle of western Europe have been affected by international pollutants.

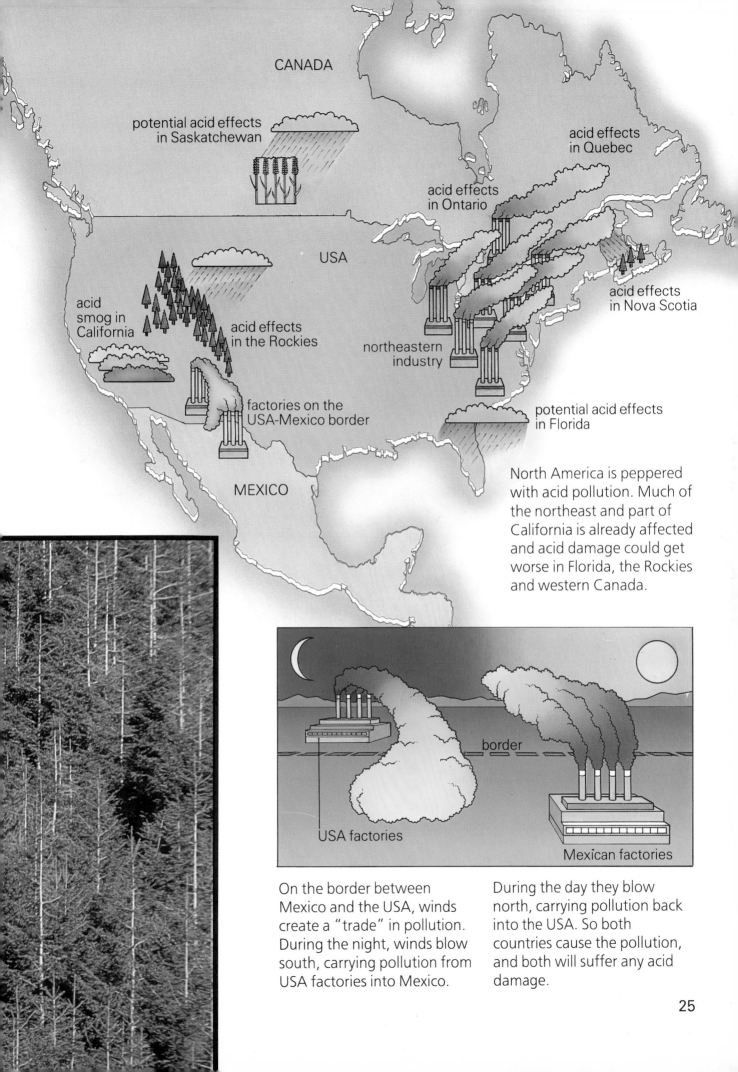

CANADA

potential acid effects
in Saskatchewan

acid effects
in Quebec

acid effects
in Ontario

USA

acid effects
in Nova Scotia

acid
smog in
California

acid effects
in the Rockies

northeastern
industry

factories on the
USA-Mexico border

potential acid effects
in Florida

MEXICO

North America is peppered
with acid pollution. Much of
the northeast and part of
California is already affected
and acid damage could get
worse in Florida, the Rockies
and western Canada.

border

USA factories

Mexican factories

On the border between
Mexico and the USA, winds
create a "trade" in pollution.
During the night, winds blow
south, carrying pollution from
USA factories into Mexico.

During the day they blow
north, carrying pollution back
into the USA. So both
countries cause the pollution,
and both will suffer any acid
damage.

25

Third World acid

Because acid pollution is largely caused by factories, it is usually associated with the industrialized countries of Europe and North America. People rarely think of it as a problem in the Third World countries of Africa, Asia and Latin America, which have fewer industries.

But as the Third World develops its own industries, so the danger of acid pollution will increase. Many Third World cities are growing rapidly, and have large numbers of vehicles that give off nitrogen oxides, causing dry acid deposition. Air pollution is already a serious problem in cities like Mexico City (Mexico), Sao Paulo (Brazil), Kuala Lumpur (Malaysia), Delhi (India), Bangkok (Thailand) and Beijing (China).

▽ Acid pollution has been reported from Brazil, Mexico, Chile and Venezuela, but few governments take the warnings seriously. Massive foreign debts make pollution control in the near future very unlikely.

▽ Africa may have little air pollution at the moment, but its effects are made more immediate since many of the poorest city dwellers live in illegal shelters on land close to industries quite unconcerned by high levels of pollution.

▽ The centers of many southeast Asian cities are warmer than the surrounding countryside. This can cause a circular airflow above the cities, creating "heat islands" that trap and circulate harmful pollutants.

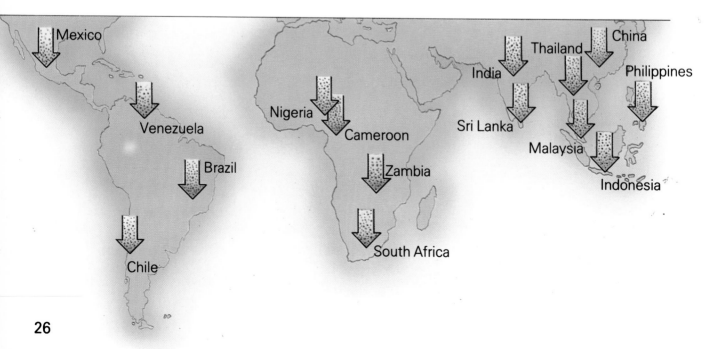

26

In countries like Zambia, South Africa, China, India and Brazil, where there are pockets of heavy industry, acid pollution is already a problem. Especially worrying is the fact that many tropical countries have soils that are particularly vulnerable to the effects of acid pollution. But unlike richer countries, those of the Third World cannot always afford the expense of reducing the emissions that cause acid pollution.

▽ Mexico City is surrounded by mountains and has little wind to disperse pollutants. Studies show that breathing the city air on the worst days has the same harmful effect as smoking two or three packs of cigarettes a day.

27

Enough!

Since it is so clearly possible that pollutant emissions can be drastically reduced, and since it is certain that high acid levels are damaging our world, why is acid rain allowed to continue to destroy our environment?

Some governments *are* concerned. To date, twenty European countries (and Canada) have agreed to take action to cut sulfur emissions by at least 30 percent by 1993 – the "30 percent Club." And they may also soon agree to control nitrogen oxide emissions.

▽ An acid pollution protest in West Germany's Black Forest. Growing public protest – and the clear evidence of swathes of dying trees – forced the West German government to agree in 1983 that urgent action was needed to control acid pollution.

But other governments – particularly those who consider themselves less affected – delay taking any action by arguing that not enough is known about the causes and effects to justify spending huge amounts of money.

So short-term economics are being weighed against the conservation and long-term health of our environment. To many, this is unacceptable, and groups of concerned people in an increasing number of countries are protesting and campaigning for better acid pollution controls.

Stop acid rain

△ This is the international symbol of the Stop Acid Rain movement. It is displayed all over the world, in many different languages.

Hard facts

Brazil

Brazil's acid pollution is worst around the big industrial areas of the southeast. Soils have been turned acid near Sao Paulo. In the nearby town of Cubatao, trees have turned to skeletons, fish die in the reddish water and human health has suffered.

Canada

Canada produces about half its own acid rain, and imports the rest from the United States. One Ontario smelter is the biggest single source of sulfur dioxide in the world. However, Canada is now pledged to a 50 percent reduction of sulfur dioxide.

China

China is the world's third largest producer of sulfur dioxide; very little of its coal is cleaned, so the smoke and ash from homes and factories make air pollution a hazard in every major city. In 1981, Shanghai had its first recorded acid rain storm.

Czechoslovakia

Air pollution has turned parts of central Czechoslovakia into ugly blots on the landscape. Illness – especially breathing problems – among children is higher than in other parts of the country. In some places, fresh water is too acid and contaminated to drink.

France

Dry acid deposition has killed trees in large areas of northern and eastern France. France has agreed to cut its sulfur dioxide emissions by half, but it may do that by expanding its nuclear power industry, which could upset environmentalists even more.

India

India is a major coal user; its annual sulfur dioxide emissions have approximately tripled in the last 20 years. Every major city in India is affected by pollution, and crops which the country can ill-afford to lose are beginning to show the signs of acid damage.

Chronology

1872 The British chemist Robert Angus Smith is the first person to describe the links between industrial emissions and acid pollution.

Early 1900s Trout become extinct in several Norwegian rivers, but the causes are unknown.

1916 Farmland downwind from a huge copper smelter in Canada is declared unfit for cultivation.

1950s and 1960s Canadian and Swedish researchers show how acid pollution can travel hundred of miles and affect soils and lakes.

1970 The Clean Air Act is implemented in the USA, establishing a national framework for air quality standards.

1973 A program is launched in 11 European countries to measure long-range air pollution.

1979 A major agreement on long-range international air pollution is signed by 35 countries in Geneva, Switzerland.

1984 West Germany announces that more than half its forests are damaged or dying. Ten countries meet in Canada and form the "30 percent Club" of countries pledged to reduce their sulfur dioxide emissions by 30 percent over ten years. More countries join later.

Japan
With all its traffic and industry, Japan once had some of the worst air pollution in the world, but stiff laws have made the air over Japanese cities considerably cleaner. But winds may be blowing acid pollution across the sea from China, bringing new problems.

Mexico
Mexico City is one of the most polluted cities in the world. Its mayor has warned of mass hysteria unless drastic measures are taken to control the pollution. Trees are dying in the city, and on some days it is impossible to see further than a few blocks.

Norway
Acid snow is a particular problem in Norway, which with its high mountains and deep fiords, is particularly vulnerable to the acid spring floods. But the Norwegian government has not yet agreed with experts that its forests are damaged.

Poland
Poland is one of the most polluted countries in the world. It burns coal that is rich in sulfur . In the most polluted regions, people suffer more illness than in other parts of the country. In the city of Crakow, even the gold roof of a chapel is dissolving.

South Africa
Coal is the main source of South African energy, and 80 percent of it is burned within 200 km (125 miles) of Johannesburg. Buildings and centuries-old rock paintings have already been damaged, and the Kruger National Park faces the threat of acid rain.

Sweden
Sweden was one of the first countries to carry out research into acid pollution, most of which it receives from other countries. More than 18,000 lakes have been acidified, and in some areas the drinking water is too polluted to give to small children.

Switzerland
Switzerland receives more air pollution from other countries than any other European country. This could prove disastrous for its forests, which cover more than a quarter of its land area. In southern parts, more than half the trees are damaged.

United Kingdom
The UK is the biggest producer of sulfur dioxide in western Europe, and upsets its European neighbors by arguing that too little is known for sure about the damage inflicted by acid pollution to justify spending money on cutting the emissions.

United States
The United States is the second biggest producer of sulfur dioxide in the world. Like the UK, it argues that too little is known about the causes of acid rain to justify spending a lot to control it. Reports of damage have come from all over the country.

USSR
The Soviet Union is the world's biggest producer of sulfur dioxide emissions, but is only prepared to reduce the pollution that is blown across its borders; what happens at home, it argues, is its own business. Even parts of Siberia may be affected.

Zambia
Copper makes up 91 percent of Zambia's exports, but the sulfur in the copper ore has led to dry deposition in and near the Zambian Copperbelt, situated in the center of the country. This could threaten freshwater fisheries, forestry and agriculture.

The Arctic
Not even the Arctic is immune from air pollution. In 1979 in the Canadian Arctic, air samples passed through experimental filters turned them gray and black. The pollution comes from the USSR, western Europe and North America.

Index

Photographic Credits:
Cover and page 24/25, Stern Magazine; page 4/5, Spectrum; page 7, Chris Howes/Seaphot; page 8, Barnaby's; page 13, Frank Spooner; page 15, Lena Skarby and page 17, Christer Agren, Swedish Environmental Research Institute; page 18, Robert Harding; page 19, Bruce Colman; pages 20 and 21, NCB; page 23, Zefa; page 27, Barry Lewis/Network; pages 28/29, John Hillelson; back cover, Susan Griggs Agency.

Acknowledgements
The publishers would like to gratefully acknowledge the valuable assistance given by Friends of the Earth and Earthscan in the preparation of this series.

WALLIS ELEMENTARY SCHOOL

proost
INTERNATIONAL BOOK PRODUCTION
PRINTED IN BELGIUM BY